EL GRECO

ABOUT THE AUTHOR

Charles Wentinck lives in France. He studied the history of art in Switzerland and in Paris. He has written books on modern painting and sculpture, and a history of European painting.

CHARLES WENTINCK

El Greco

BARNES & NOBLE, INC.

NEW YORK

Publishers • Booksellers • Since 1873

Editor: Anthony Bosman

Translation: Albert J. Fransella

Lay-out: Wim van Stek

Published in the United States in 1964

by Barnes & Noble, Inc., 105 Fifth Avenue, New York 3, N.Y.

© 1963 and printed in Holland by The Ysel Press Ltd, Deventer

EL GRECO

It may well be that the time is past when one could
write about El Greco in a manner so very different
from the way one approached other painters. Writing
about El Greco used to be looked upon as a profession
of faith. The least requirement that had to be satisfied
was a pilgrimage to Toledo and only after "noches
toledanas" would the historian be able to discover the
secret of El Greco's art.

One of the most sensational experiences, at the begin-
ning of the present century, was the conversion of Julius
Meier-Graefe, for his encounter with El Greco cannot
be described by any other term. Meier-Graefe was
possessed of an unusually lively intellect, coupled with
a lordly bearing. His explorations in the field of art
history seldom remained within the bounds of scholarly
propriety. His knowledge was based upon what he saw
with his own eyes, and he changed his mind, which he
never allowed to become prejudiced, whenever what
he saw gave cause for changing it.

In 1908 he went to Spain to see the works of Velázquez. When he first set foot in the Prado, Madrid's
great museum, in search of the Master he so much
admired, he dismissed the El Grecos as "drunken fan-

tasies". He had come solely to see the great, the one and only, Velázquez. But in the gallery, surrounded by the works of Velázquez, he felt no impact. He failed to respond to the spell of the genius he had considered one of the six greatest painters of all time. His appreciation of the pictorial ability of Velázquez remained, but what troubled him was a feeling that the impression Velázquez made on the outside world was being repeated with him. Vision was lacking.

And then, in the home of Beruete, he was shown the latter's El Grecos. They surpassed all his expectations. No forms were there which could be judged on a basis of realism. Now Meier-Graefe defined the art of Velázquez—most unjustly—as "consummate craftsmanship, talent at its best, but without genius". All at once the great qualities possessed by Velázquez paled into insignificance beside the newly discovered greatness of El Greco.

"What Rembrandt sought in shadows, El Greco was able to produce in bright colours, in the light red of Renoir, in the purple of Cézanne, in the white of Manet." These are the words of a man who, schooled in the art of his time, saw everything with his own eyes. A man who was one of the first to write the history of the artists just mentioned. And a man who, since then, has found in the Old Masters what the young ones taught him to see. All the discoveries of the moderns—colour in the shadows, blurring of outlines, the combination of tonality and contrast—all these are to be found in El Greco. An eye, an eyelid, an eye socket painted like a landscape: that was Cézanne, who created form out of colour.

One of Meier-Graefe's implicit convictions was that the art of the past may be understood better the more carefully one studies the work of the moderns. This belief is supported by his writings, in particular the account of his Spanish journey, which tells of his discovery of El Greco. He realised earlier than others where the significance of this painter lay. Earlier, and more deeply, because the French art of the nineteenth century and the German art of the twentieth century had so broadened his vision that the work of El Greco now came within his compass.

It was not a gradual conquest, nor was it a slow conversion. No; it was as though an act of grace had suddenly opened his eyes at the very moment when he thought that all his great discoveries and experiences lay behind him. He had supposed that he had already absorbed everything of any real importance and that all that was left for him to do would be the sorting, amplifying and classifying of fellow travellers and of disciples.

At this moment El Greco appeared to him, like a revelation. He confessed that ever since his school days he had acknowledged only three "continents": Michelangelo, Rubens and Rembrandt. Now there was a fourth. And that no island, lying lost somewhere in an ocean; no-

peninsula, attached to the mainland. No—a real, new, immense continent, just as important as the other three! In the joy of his discovery, he called upon his contemporaries to make up for their negligence and make recompense for the neglect of millions of people for some three hundred years.

Since then, the renown of El Greco has grown apace; he has taken his place among the classical masters of Spanish painting, though not quite the one allotted him by the enthusiastic Meier-Graefe. However, for many he is not only a great but a mysterious and fascinating master, whose art is unique and has never been equalled; whose image as a man and as a world figure is not derived from that of anyone else; whose style anticipated that of the centuries following him. Above all, he is the man whose genius—expressed in its full force in his paintings—has always remained fascinating because, more than those of any other Spanish painter, his works expressed the feelings of a people—a people to whom he did not actually belong.

Kyriakos (or Domenikos) Theotokopoulos (in Spanish, Domingo Teotocopuli) is known in the history of Spanish art as "El Greco" (The Greek). A Byzantine Greek, born on the island of Crete in the 1540's, he spent some years of his youth in Venice in the 60's, left there for Rome about 1570, and turned up in Spain about 1567. His Byzantine characteristics showed themselves in his fondness for solemn religious ceremonial.

In his pictures the lack of spatiality recalls memories of the two-dimensional mosaics of Byzantium.

In Venice, where he came under the influence of the municipal school of painting, the suggestion of spatiality customary there forced him to the third dimension. That he studied under Titian is confirmed by a letter of recommendation from Giulio Clovio, addressed to Cardinal Farnese. In view of the known date of his residence in the city of lagoons, El Greco could well have witnessed how the aged Titian painted "Crowning with Thorns" which now hangs in the Pinakothek in Munich.

The later Titians indicate the new path which the work of El Greco follows: a style of painting from which line drawing has been eliminated and in which the purely pictorial is to dominate. Colour no longer suffers any limitation; nor is it any longer necessary to indicate where one colour begins and the other ends. El Greco's paintings are the irrefutable documentary proofs of his association with Titian. El Greco's "Golgotha" (p. 31) in the Prado shows a definite similarity to Titian's "Golgotha" in Ancona. The "Magdalen" paintings and the portraits of the "Salvator Mundi" by El Greco also demonstrate in what ways and to what extent he was influenced by his great master. Furthermore, El Greco's "Descent of the Holy Ghost" (pp. 58, 59), in the Prado, distinctly recalls the famous painting by Titian in the Church of Santa Maria della Salute in Venice.

The influence of the Venetian school on El Greco, however, was by no means confined to that of Titian. In his portraits El Greco used Veronese and Tintoretto as models for his style. He was also impressed by the work of Jacopo Bassano. The extent of his contact with Bassano is debatable, but in the brushwork, and certainly in the colouring, the work of the young El Greco does remind one of that of Bassano, especially in the way he produced his lighting effects.

From Venice, El Greco went to Parma to see the work of Correggio, and in 1570 he found himself in Rome. By this time his pictorial preference was determined: he was to assume the heritage of the Venetian school.

"A young fellow from Candia has made his appearance in Rome, a pupil of Titian; he appears to me to be an excellent painter. Among other things, he has painted a self-portrait which has created a sensation among all the artists in Rome." So begins a letter from Clovio to Cardinal Alessandro Farnese, who immediately offered El Greco an apartment in his palace until the painter could establish himself. In token of gratitude, El Greco painted, very much in the Tintoretto tradition, the portrait of Giulio Clovio (p. 37).

To a painter of the Venetian school, Raphael could offer very little. El Greco did view Raphael's works in the Vatican, but he was not very appreciative of the classical balance and the linear limitations of this type of art. For him, these paintings were only witnesses to a grand but irrevocable past.

There is not a single document in existence to indicate what El Greco did, with whom he came into contact, or what befell him during his years in Rome.

One figure only stands out as having been of decisive significance for El Greco. The work of no other artist was so clearly significant of things to come as that of Michelangelo, who, in the last period of his work, had turned away from the art of the Renaissance, with its formal idealisation of nature and its imitative basis. He replaced its objective representation of the world by an artistic conception which places psychic emotions and experiences above fidelity to sense perceptions. His art had, in fact, become anaturalistic. Here is his point of contact with El Greco: it is from him that El Greco adopted the anaturalism of his forms, just as he had learned the art of anaturalistic colouring and composition from Tintoretto—who had likewise acquired these new conceptions from Michelangelo. Both these influences may be evaluated as contributing to an explanation of El Greco's Toledo style.

The susceptibility of El Greco to anaturalism was by no means a mere matter of concern for form, any more than the anaturalism of Michelangelo and Tintoretto could be explained as a purely stylistic phenomenon. The basis of the style designated as "mannerism"— heralded by Michelangelo and Tintoretto—is to be

11

found in a "spiritualism" born of the spiritual in-
security of that period. A shift in emphasis was taking
place from the outer to the inner beauty. This is most
strongly expressed in the later drawings of Christ by
Michelangelo.

Probably, however, El Greco was more deeply influenced by French than by Italian mannerism. The
slender, elongated figures with the small, gracefully
inclined heads, the glances laden with emotion and the
nervous hands—typical of Jacques Bellange—are all to be
found in El Greco. According to the painter Dvorák,
the art of the French mannerists provided El Greco with
something the Italians were unable to give him: the
conception of a complete victory over the world by
withdrawal into one's inner self.

After 1590, El Greco's conversion to a wholly inward
expression was complete. This expressionism achieved
its consummation in works such as the "View of
Toledo" (p. 62) and the "Vision of St. John the Divine"
(pp. 51, 52, 53).

Characteristic of this late style is the anaturalistic
anatomy of the human figures, seen in the "Vision of
St. John the Divine". The proportion between head and
body has little relation to reality. Form has freed itself
from corporeal actuality; it has become the embodiment
of a psychical rather than a physical reality. It owes its
existence to the imagination, and not to imitation.
Light and colour both contribute towards the spiritual-

Probably a self-portrait of El Greco as a nobleman in the
"Burial of Count Orgaz"; 1586; Church of SanTomé, Toledo

isation of the form. Never before in Europe had there been an art so anticlassical as that of El Greco, so far removed from reality.

From various quarters efforts have been made to associate this spiritualisation with the religious currents which dominated those times. Kehrer saw in El Greco's "Auflösung der Form" (dissolution of form) a pictorial parallel with the "Auflösung des Eigenwillens" (dissolution of one's own will) as demanded by Ignatius of Loyola in his "Exercitia Spiritualia". The mysticism of John of the Cross (born in Toledo in 1542) and that of St. Theresa (who died in 1582) or that of her spiritual guide, Pedro de Alcántara, have all been brought into relation with El Greco. It has even been conjectured that the painter had been initiated into the secrets of cabalism —a supposition which rests upon the high regard the mysticism of the cabala enjoyed at the time in Old Castile and in Toledo.

Be that as it may, it would have been very difficult for El Greco's mystical tendencies to develop while he was in Rome. Indeed, Rome had ceased to be the spiritual centre of the world. Christendom was experiencing its renaissance elsewhere, in the land of the Alumbrados (Enlightened Ones), of St. Ignatius, of St. Theresa of Avila; in the land where—despite the Renaissance— people still built and felt on Gothic lines, and where the mysticism of the Middle Ages, combined with psychic inwardness, still blazed; in the Spain where the

Escorial had been erected as a new stronghold for the Faith and where the palaces of Toledo had been converted into cloisters.

The absence of any and all naturalistic conditioning of thought and feeling was characteristic of the Spain of those days. "What I see," said St. Theresa, "is a white and a red such as one finds nowhere in nature, which shine and glow more brightly than anything else one can perceive, and images which no artist has yet painted, the originals of which are nowhere to be found, and which nevertheless are nature itself and life itself and the loveliest beauty that can be imagined."

It was in the manner in which this saint experienced her ecstasies that El Greco endeavoured to paint. Subjective spiritual experience became for him the sole basis for psychic exaltation. In Italy and in France artists were still harnessed to objectivity in the treatment of figures. In Spain they were even prepared to sacrifice the last remnants of the Renaissance conception of truth and beauty. "St. Joseph with the Child Jesus" (p. 45), with the choir of angels above the head of the Saint, is no longer the representation of a person in the style of which a thousand artists before El Greco and thousands more after him were capable. This portrait is not based upon the imitation of reality, but is the creation of an inner voice. In the same way, the portrait of Guevara, the Grand Inquisitor (p. 41) is not so much the portrayal of a particular person as that of the embodiment of the *idea* of the "Grand Inquisitor", almost as we know him from Dostoevski, as Fate incarnate.

It is not difficult, therefore, to guess why El Greco went to Toledo. When, during a lawsuit, the question was put to him, what had brought him to Toledo, he replied: "I am not compelled to render any account of my reasons for coming to this city." But a description of the Toledo of those days satisfactorily answers the question:

"This Spanish Lhasa, which at that time housed a hundred and fifty thousand people, contained hundreds of cloisters, to which new ones were added every year. Laws promulgated against them were of no effect. Toledo was, it is true, a busy place, but all its industry was centred around the palace of the Archbishop, who was, after the Emperor, the most powerful man in the country; around the thousand cloisters in which they were concerned, not for the living, but only for the dead; around the Puerta del Cambrón, the court of the Tribunal of the Inquisition. For Toledo, this mighty spiritual fortress, was waging war for God against the rest of the world."

Until comparatively recently, Toledo retained this character of a bulwark of intolerant fanaticism. The city itself resembled an immense cathedral, where the people went hungry in the midst of treasures which did not belong to them but to Heaven. Priests, monks and nuns, oblivious of the problems and contrasts of real life, still strode through the streets as in the days of Ignatius of Loyola. Even in the twenties of our present century there were still no newspapers, no street lamps. It was as though there was a deliberate intention to preserve, artificially, the darkness of the Middle Ages.

It was here in this city that El Greco became the painter we know. Monks, priests and inquisitors saw themselves for the first time in the portraits he painted: sombre, serious men, whose dignity had acquired the quality of asceticism and contempt for the world. In the archives of a nunnery the following reference to El Greco was found: "He came to us in order to paint the altar of Santo Domingo."

With his "El Espolio" (pp. 22, 23, 24) the doors of the Cathedral opened for him. El Greco has filled the whole surface of this painting with figures. The abstract foundation—in which ultimately the strength of every picture lies—with its shallow planes cutting across one another, makes one think more of a modern painting than of a work of the sixteenth century. The conflicting accentuation of these planes, and the manner in which they make their appearance in close formation one after the other, directs the eye to the red plane in the centre. "El Espolio" (The Despoiling of Christ) pictures the moment when Christ is on the point of being deprived of his splendid earthly attire, which is at the same time the symbol of his kingship. People crowd around him. Two of them are looking in the direction of the viewer, and appear to be functioning as go-betweens: a stupid soldier who does not know what to think about it all and a somewhat older executioner who is pointing imperiously towards Jesus. Some of the others are just brutes who obviously take delight in persecution; mostly, however, they are ordinary people from the streets of Toledo. The terrifying quality of this painting lies in the tightly packed mass of people, who are gripped with anger because Christ is not as they are.

Noteworthy, also, are the apparent apathy and aloofness in their faces. The face of Christ reveals the distance which, inwardly, he already feels between himself and his surroundings. His eyes seem to be fixed upon another world, and his left hand is even bestowing a blessing upon the executioner's servant who is preparing the cross.

From then on, the attention of Philip the Second was fixed upon El Greco. On April 23, 1580, he commissioned a picture with the theme of the "Martyrdom of St. Maurice" (p. 26); it was to be delivered by August 17, 1584. But the King refused to accept the painting. And so the career of court painter, which had seemed to lie before El Greco, eluded him.

His renown, however, was not lessened by Philip's rejection. In 1586 he painted, for the Church of San Tomé, the "Burial of Count Orgaz" (pp. 29, 30, 39), the painting with which he terminated his first Toledo period. The entire surface of this picture is filled with

18

(Continued on page 73)

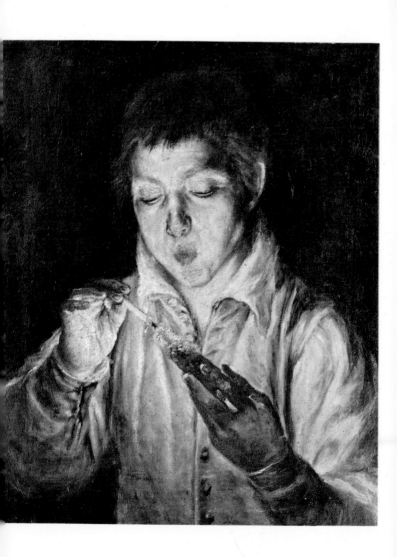

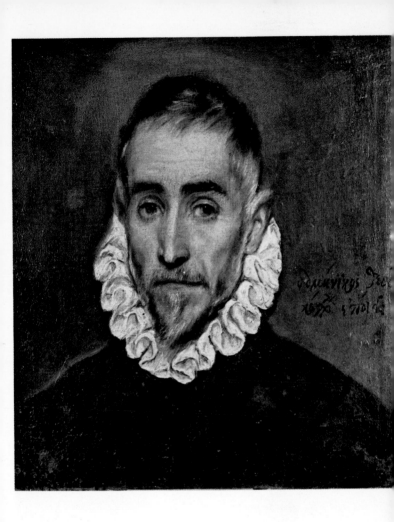

figures; Heaven and Earth are bound together, both rhythmically and structurally, into a unity. The profile of the praying monk behind the boy with the torch sets this rhythm, which carries along with it the group around the dead Count, and comes to an end with the dramatic figure, seen from the back, of the priest, who is staring ecstatically into the beyond. The figures surrounding the body of the Count are carried upwards to celestial glory, and in this way Heaven and Earth are brought together. Mary is waiting to receive the soul of the dead man from the hands of the Archangel. Seldom before have so many figures been portrayed together in one painting: in all, twenty-three heads of priests, monks, Knights of Calatrava and learned men. The brothers Covarrubias can be identified, as well as El Greco himself—whose face is more brightly lighted than those of the other men in the foreground. The boy with the torch is the eight-year-old son of the painter.

After this work, El Greco received commission after commission. Into his art he introduced religion and the Church, mysticism and doctrine. He painted innumerable portraits. Women seldom appear in his work. Only once did he paint the portrait of a living female, his daughter; it was almost always princes of the Church, priests and monks. All were servants of a theocracy in which the fanatical spirit of the Inquisition reigned and in which any supposed treachery to God was severely punished. The belief in God was just as unshakable as in the betrayal perpetrated upon Him, and avenging justice saw to it that punishment was cruel.

Christ was conceived of as a warrior, in the spirit of Ignatius of Loyola. Round him were arrayed the saints, like fallen soldiers of the Faith, and the vision of their resurrection lived on in the hearts of the Spanish people.

As with every strong belief, this too gave birth to an equally strong art. It was not a belief in beauty, as in Italy, but a belief in holiness. And it was as visions of holiness become flesh that the figures of the saints were created.

The city, too, was more a vision than a reality. It appeared in El Greco's paintings as a Gethsemane; above the ash-grey, barren land hang clouds torn like the curtain of which it is written that in the hour of Christ's death it was rent in twain. The "View of Toledo" (p. 62) is not the picture of a landscape, but the outcry of a soul gripped by the demonic powers of nature; it is self-revelation, self-recognition in the grand spectacle before which everything earthly pales into insignificance.

The first portrait El Greco painted in Toledo which is characteristic of his style, was the "Portrait of a Nobleman with a Sword" (p. 38), in the Prado. It would seem to have been done not long after "El Espolio", and gives a direct impression of the stiff haughtiness of the Spanish nobility. The silence which prevails in this portrait is that of the dead. Also in the Prado is another portrait of an unknown nobleman, which is limited to the head alone (p. 36). The eyes show the intermingling of melancholy and religious introspection so frequently to be seen; the subject is detached in mind from the here and now, and intolerant in the rigidity of a stern creed. Magnificent is the "Portrait of Cardinal Don Fernando Nino de Guevara" (p. 41). One who stands in front of this canvas almost fears that he is one of the accused. The look in the eyes of this judge portends the inescapable torture chamber. In his full official robes, Spain's most hated man sits enthroned in the marble hall of his palace; the cold, inexorable eyes behind the spectacles direct a piercing gaze upon the condemned. The thin lips are compressed into a sharp line cut into his parchment countenance.

Other portraits of sitting figures followed. "Brother Hortensio Felix Paravicino" (p. 65) was the man who wrote the sonnet for El Greco's tomb. He was already a professor at the University of Salamanca when he was only twenty-one years of age. El Greco depicts him sitting in the auditorium, with a folio in his lap and one finger stuck between the pages of a small book; a sharp-witted man, a man worth listening to.

Like Rembrandt in Amsterdam, El Greco dwelt in the Jewish quarter of his city. He had taken up his abode in a part of the palace of the Marqués de Villena. Toledo was more congenial to him than Rome, for here he found once again not only the pines and the olive trees of the isle of his birth, but also the buildings, the songs and the customs of the Mohammedan East.

Little is known of El Greco's comings and goings in Toledo. He particularly endeavoured not to draw attention to himself, he was obedient towards authority and he attended church faithfully. It was only on those evenings when he was visited by Covarrubias (p. 42)—a man known to be a friend of the Greeks—that he conducted himself in a less inhibited manner. On such occasions he would sometimes give full vent to his scorn for everything that was not Greek. In his opinion, the Spaniards were inferior even to the Italians, whom he regarded as no better than the proletarians who lived in the suburbs of Athens. Anyone who dared to make the remark that Greece was only a small and insignificant country was soon to hear that when Spain no longer counted, Hellas would still be a power in the world, unassailable by emperors or clergy. And moreover, he would go on to say, in four or five hundred years' time Spain would have to thank that same power, Hellas, for its only remaining renown, which would be based on the fact that the last of the Greeks, Theotokopoulos, born in Crete, and called El Greco, had been so gracious as to have painted a few pictures in Spain. On such occasions he used to speak only Greek, and the learned Covarrubias would listen with attention and pleasure. From the inventory of El Greco's estate, we learn that among the authors he read were Homer, Euripides, Demosthenes, Lucian and Aesop—the heritage of Antiquity.

El Greco's own inheritance from Greece is apparent in his "Martyrdom of St. Maurice" (pp. 26, 28). The bodies in this painting are as plastic as those in an antique relief. Their beauty has the innate nobility of Antiquity, a beauty from before the Fall of Man. Naked stride the figures of the Theban Legion, a multitude destined to die. The bigoted King Philip the Second did not know what to make of this pagan joy in nudity; according to the historian Sigüenza, the painting did not please His Majesty.

The "Laocoön" (p. 68) also portrays the naked body in its emphatic corporeality. In this picture the male figure acquires such a vital intensity that, as Vasari wrote, it "does not appear to be painted; it seems to be alive."

Nudity is even more powerfully represented in the figures of the martyrs in the "Vision of St. John the Divine" (pp. 51, 52, 53), with its Apocalyptic motif, and its passionate and tragic earnestness. The martyrs, having heard the wild call that makes the world tremble, cry out, "How long, O Lord?" The violent gestures of the arms stretched heavenwards write their tragic message against just such a sky as arches itself above Toledo in the painting, done about 1608, called "View of Toledo" (p. 62). In this picture the darkness of the night covers the landscape; the earth trembles, flashes of lightning trace their flaming tracks, clouds race past. Fear of the unknown, of the mysterious and demonic character of nature, seizes the spectator. It is the landscape of an apocalypse, of a destruction of the worlds. Man becomes lost in nature; nature itself becomes the battlefield of human passions. Form dissolves into light; shrubs flicker like flames; rocks lose their angularity. Things are stripped of their definiteness, and seem to serve only as the revelation of a visionary experience.

In these paintings El Greco's work moves a long way from the baroque. What still connects him in some way with it is his fondness for movement. But what differentiates him is his subjectivity, the genuinely irrational character of his ecstatic visions. Aldous Huxley, in a remarkable essay on El Greco, pointed out that the Jesuits had devised a technique for the unlimited mass production of religious ecstasy. In so doing, they altered into cheap sentimentality what had hitherto been accessible to, and dearly paid for by, a religiously gifted nature, and had brought it within the reach of all; they transformed the sublime, by the external devices of theatrical glances and emotional gestures into the commonplace. From then on, any painter, however dull-spirited he might be, could manufacture some sort of religious art.

El Greco was almost the only artist who refused to paint the heavens as reassuring, the saints as human, all-

Probably a self-portrait of El Greco
1605-10; 23¼ × 18¼ in.; The Metropolitan Museum of Art,
New York (Joseph Pulitzer Bequest)

too-human, and the sacraments as commonplace, because with him, ecstasy was a personal, bodily experience, immediate in the strictly physiological sense. In his "Resurrection of Christ" (pp. 56, 57) Christ is shown as having arisen from a welter of herculean figures, whose turbulent limbs coil themselves like the flames from which the phoenix arose. Bewilderment stares from the eyes of those fettered to the earth; sword and dagger appear impotent against the miracle.

In the "Adoration of the Shepherds" (pp. 71, 72) the shepherds appear superhuman; their gigantic figures surpass all natural proportions. But deep is their humility after what they have experienced in the night. The shepherd in the centre is on his knees to behold the miracle of the Birth, while the figure farthest to the left shrinks back in wonder and awe. Above the stable, a shaft of light breaks a path from the heavens. Angels proclaim their gladness, not as ethereal mythical beings, but as real, living messengers travelling back and forth between Heaven and Earth.

Sometimes, in El Greco's work, there is a loveliness to be found closely akin to that of Correggio or of Parmigianino—for example, in "The Holy Family" in the Cleveland Museum of Art (pp. 54, 55). But in the colouring, something takes place which did not happen in Italy: a fabulous orchestration of purple and blue, of yellow and green, gives the folds of the garments a life-like movement very similar to that of the clouds marching along overhead in a sky that only El Greco could paint.

There is an incredibly bold distortion of form in the "Assumption of the Virgin Mary" (p. 69) in the Museum of San Vicente at Toledo. Grandiose is the figure of the Angel, an incarnated impulse raised heavenwards with a mystical gesture by Mary. The wings are painted in an unimaginably simple manner—black and white on a red background—but owe their mighty expressiveness to this very simplicity, which enabled the brush to delineate such power and rapture.

El Greco has freed the saints from the traditional burial scene in iconography. He portrays St. Andrew and St. Francis as rising up on either side of an X-shaped cross against a troubled sky (p. 67). They stretch upwards, as though yearning for Heaven, in Gothic slenderness; their ascetic and nervous hands evoke, rather than describe, eloquent, though restrained, gestures.

St. Francis, in his mind already withdrawn from earthly life, holds in his hands a skull, which sets Death before his very eyes (p. 66). Death, which signifies to him fulfillment rather than negation. Hence his look, which has nothing of fear but everything of respect, almost of friendliness, towards this most certain of all certainties.

St. Dominic, we see (p. 61) absorbed in an ecstasy of prayer, amid bare plains, which accentuate his immeas-

81

urable solitude—immeasurable but not comfortless. For against the rock rests the image of the Crucified One, and in the inward gaze of the Saint the mystical union becomes an accomplished fact.

The typically Spanish longing for miracles is expressed in every legend of Spain. The Spanish kings had themselves buried wearing the cowl of the Dominicans. Charles the Fifth renounced his throne in order to die in a monastery. In a procession, Philip the Second bore on his own shoulders the relics of the saints. This passion, this closeness to the world beyond, is also expressed in El Greco's portraits of the saints.

It is this possession by visions, this dream-ridden intensity, which determines the position El Greco occupies in the art of his century. What was merely pictorial and decorative with other painters, became symbolical and expressionistic with El Greco. He was to be the first to throw over the fundamentals of classicism. He considered the plane more important than the suggestion of depth, and colouring more important than line. In the construction of his composition he allowed psychic necessity to prevail over the realistic truth sanctioned by academic convention. Light was to model the form, just as with the masters of the nineteenth century. The essential received the markedly suggestive accent, as with the masters of the twentieth century. The intensity with which El Greco practised the vibrating rhythm of line heralded the painting of Van Gogh.

Only a very great painter could take the liberties El Greco permitted himself. Often a single stroke of his brush depicts the fall of a garment, the expression of a face, the structure of a hand or a foot. And as a colourist he availed himself of remarkable combinations of light blue and lemon yellow which were unique in his century.

It is to all these elements that El Greco owes his significance. Seldom in the history of the art of painting has a blaze of imagination such as his been attended by so much pictorial boldness.

LIST OF ILLUSTRATIONS

Except for "Mount Sinai" (p. 19), all the works listed below were painted in oils on canvas.

The pictures reproduced on pages 36-44 provide a review of El Greco's art in portraiture.

26 MARTYRDOM OF ST. MAURICE
1580; 174$\frac{3}{8}$ × 118$\frac{7}{8}$ in.;
Chapter Hall, El Escorial, near Madrid.
The legend of St. Maurice tells how he, as Commander-in-Chief of the Theban Legion, consisting mainly of Egyptian Christians, was dispatched to Gaul by the Roman Emperor Diocletian to persecute the Christians. St. Maurice and the Legion refused to take prisoner and kill their fellow believers. Then they themselves underwent this fate at the hands of the Romans.

27 THE DREAM OF PHILIP II
1580; 55$\frac{1}{8}$ × 43$\frac{1}{4}$ in.;
Chapter Hall, El Escorial, near Madrid

28 Detail of the MARTYRDOM OF ST. MAURICE (see 26)
Roman soldiers and executioners with the decapitated body of St. Maurice

29 BURIAL OF COUNT ORGAZ
1586; 189 × 141$\frac{3}{4}$ in.; Church of San Tomé, Toledo

30 Detail of the BURIAL OF COUNT ORGAZ (see 29)
St. Stephen and St. Augustine with the dead Count Orgaz

31 GOLGOTHA
About 1590; 122$\frac{7}{8}$ × 66$\frac{1}{2}$ in.; Prado, Madrid

32 Detail of GOLGOTHA (see 31)
The Mater Dolorosa

33 CHRIST CARRYING THE CROSS
About 1595; 42$\frac{1}{4}$ × 34$\frac{5}{8}$ in.; Prado, Madrid

34 Detail of THE HOLY FAMILY: The Virgin Mary
About 1598; 44$\frac{1}{8}$ × 41$\frac{1}{4}$ in.;
Hospitium de San Juan Bautista, Toledo

46 THE TWO SAINTS JOHN (John the Evangelist and John the Baptist)
About 1608; $42\frac{7}{8} \times 33\frac{1}{2}$ in.;
Church of the Jesuits, Toledo

47 Detail of THE TWO SAINTS JOHN (see 46)
John the Baptist

48 BAPTISM OF CHRIST
About 1598; $137\frac{3}{4} \times 56\frac{3}{4}$; Prado, Madrid

49 BAPTISM OF CHRIST
About 1612-14; $162 \times 76\frac{3}{4}$ in.;
Hospitium de San Juan Bautista, Toledo

50 Detail of the BAPTIST OF CHRIST (see 49)
Christ kneeling

51 VISION OF ST. JOHN THE DIVINE
1610-14; $88\frac{1}{2} \times 76$ in.; The Metropolitan Museum of Art, New York (Rogers Fund, 1956)
Revelation 6: 9-11: "And when he had opened the fifth seal, I saw under the altar the souls of them that were slain for the word of God, and for the testimony which they held: And they cried with a loud voice, saying, How long, O Lord, holy and true, dost thou not judge and avenge our blood on them that dwell on the earth? And white robes were given unto every one of them; and it was said unto them, that they should rest yet for a little season, until their fellow servants also and their brethren, that should be killed as they were, should be fulfilled."

52 Detail of the VISION OF ST. JOHN THE DIVINE (see 51)

53 Detail of the VISION OF ST. JOHN THE DIVINE (see 51)
St. John

54 Detail of THE HOLY FAMILY (see 55)
Head of the Virgin Mary. It is believed that Doña Jerónima de las Cuebas was the model.

55 THE HOLY FAMILY
1592-96; $51\frac{7}{8} \times 39\frac{1}{2}$ in.;
The Cleveland Museum of Art, Cleveland, Ohio (gift of the Friends of the Cleveland Museum of Art, 1926)

56 RESURRECTION OF CHRIST
1597-1604; $108\frac{1}{4} \times 50$ in.; Prado, Madrid

57 Detail of the RESURRECTION OF CHRIST (see 56)
Frightened soldiers

58 Detail of the DESCENT OF THE HOLY GHOST (see 59)
The Virgin Mary with a woman standing at her side. This woman, who is not mentioned in the history of the Apostles, was probably taken by El Greco from a painting by Titian which is in the Church of Santa Maria della Salute in Venice.

59 DESCENT OF THE HOLY GHOST
1604-12; $108\frac{1}{4} \times 50$ in.; Prado, Madrid
According to various historians, the "Resurrection of Christ" and the "Descent of the Holy Ghost" were painted as companion pieces, though the "Descent" must have been painted several years later than the "Resurrection".

60 ST. MARTIN AND THE BEGGAR
1597-99; $75\frac{1}{4} \times 38\frac{5}{8}$ in.;
National Gallery of Art, Washington (Widener Collection)

61 ST. DOMINIC
About 1604; $47\frac{1}{4} \times 22\frac{7}{8}$ in.; The Cathedral, Toledo

62 VIEW OF TOLEDO
About 1608; $47\frac{5}{8} \times 22\frac{7}{8}$ in.; The Metropolitan Museum of Art, New York (bequest of Mrs. H. O. Havemeyer, 1929)
The H. O. Havemeyer Collection

63 THE HOLY FAMILY
About 1598; $42\frac{1}{8} \times 27\frac{1}{8}$ in.; Prado, Madrid